Out of the Dark Night

Out of the Dark Night

A Collection of Short Stories from Asia

Hat Muoi

Out of the Dark Night
Copyright © 2013 by Hat Muoi

Published 2013 by Graceworks Private Limited
7 Eng Kong Terrace
Singapore 598979
E-mail: enquiries@graceworks.com.sg
Website: www.graceworks.com.sg

Unless otherwise indicated, all Scripture quotations are taken from THE HOLY BIBLE, NEW INTERNATIONAL VERSION®, NIV® copyright © 1973, 1978, 1984, 2011 by Biblica, Inc.™ Used by permission. All rights reserved worldwide.

Scripture quotations marked "NCV" are taken from the New Century Version. Copyright © 1987, 1988, 1991 by Word Publishing, a division of Thomas Nelson Inc. Used by permission. All rights reserved.

A CIP catalogue record for this book is available from the National Library of Singapore.

Design by Intent Design
Cover photo courtesy of Annette Chen

ISBN: 978-981-07-6659-7

Printed in Singapore

1 2 3 4 5 6 7 8 9 10 • 21 20 19 18 17 16 15 14 13

Contents

Foreword

When I first met Esther nine years ago, she was publishing books that had been translated from English to Vietnamese. Then she attended our LittWorld 2004 conference in the Philippines and caught the vision for publishing Vietnamese writers, not just translations. She could see a place for translating good Christian books from English or other languages. But what if she were to publish original material — stories and messages by Vietnamese writers, written in the heart language and rooted in the culture of her readers? Wouldn't these works have a greater potential of connecting with readers and impacting hearts and lives?

Esther set to work. She and a team of volunteers conceived the idea of starting a women's magazine. They received training at an MAI writers' workshop in 2008, and within weeks launched the inaugural issue of *Hat Muoi* ("Grain of Salt"). All 2,000 copies of this Christmas 2008 issue quickly sold out, as did the 3,000 copies of the Easter 2009 issue. Seeing the demand, Esther and her team raised the print run to 4,000 for the third issue, and to 8,000 for the fourth. The magazine's first-person testimonies always attracted lots of reader interest.

Over the past few years, we sent gifted trainers Bernice Lee of Singapore and Ramon Rocha of the Philippines to help Esther and her team equip local writers and editors for the magazine. At one of these trainings, an idea was shared:

What if we gathered some of the best testimonies from the magazine and published them as a book?

That is exactly what happened.

This book, which you hold in your hands, shares story after story of God's remarkable power to shine the light of hope in the darkest circumstances. Writers tell in gritty detail their battles with depression, sickness, addiction, indebtedness, and even insanity; and how their personal encounter with Jesus Christ gloriously transformed everything. It is impossible to read these despair-to-joy stories and remain unmoved.

After Jesus healed a man possessed with demons, the man wanted to *do* something. Jesus simply said, "Go home to your family and tell them how much the Lord has done for you and how he has had mercy on you" (Mark 5:19, NCV). I am thankful that the writers in *Out of the Dark Night* have observed Jesus' mandate and told of what He has done for them. I am especially thankful that with this English-language edition, non-Vietnamese readers can now read and benefit from these stories.

Might Esther and her team have imagined that one day, instead of translating books from the West, they would see their material translated into English? Thank God it has indeed happened.

John Maust

President,
Media Associates International

Holding her hand, I thanked God for giving me this opportunity to know such a special individual.

He Raised Me Up

Dinh Tran, based on the testimony of Xuan Ha

"Iced tea! Iced tea, anyone?"

The cry of the little, dark-skinned girl was drowned by the noise of the bustling Cho-Lon Market. Weaving through the throngs of people each day with her tiny pitcher of iced tea, she tried to make a living at marketplaces and bus stations, not just to feed herself but also to make ends meet for her little siblings at home.

Every sunset after gathering all the tea cans, she continued to make her rounds through the fabric outlets with a basketful of tangerines. She was smart, agile, and hardworking, but all these qualities combined were not enough to help the girl rise above her unfortunate fate.

With the same set of old, faded clothes and a worn-out pair of flip-flops, barely held together with metal wires after falling apart several times, she fought her way through life day in and day out. She suppressed her craving to indulge in some cookies or sweet soup so that she could save money to feed her family. All that she was able to satiate herself with was a bowl of rice with some broth and soy sauce sprinkled on top. Once in a while, she would build up the courage to ask the vendor for some extra broth but these requests were angrily rebuffed with: "You always ask for more broth when you can only afford rice!" The world kept turning, life went on, and no one ever noticed the poor girl eating from her tear-filled bowl of rice.

When she was only six, she had to witness the separation of her parents. She and her younger siblings stayed with their mother but instead of being looked after, the children often found themselves abandoned as their mother was constantly away, dabbling in sorcery and other dark arts.

At the age of seven, while all her peers were going to school, the girl found herself lost in the school of life, crying out to strangers in the marketplace in an attempt to sell various foodstuffs. After turning ten, she had to taste the harshness of being a housemaid so that she could provide for her family. Her poor childhood knew nothing of a decent meal or nice clothing and, because of the heavy load of responsibility on her shoulders, even a lunchtime nap was too much to hope for.

The end of her unfortunate childhood was the start of even more difficult teenage years. She can never forget the days of "train hopping" at Binh Trieu station where every afternoon she would have to crawl through holes and wait for passing trains to jump onto. While hiding on top of the train, she had to withstand the blazing heat of day and cutting cold of night, always fighting to stay awake so she wouldn't fall off or get smashed when the train moved through a tunnel. As she continued to grow, so too did the hardship in her life and she soon found herself the only female bus attendant at Long Khanh station, carrying and moving heavy loads like any of the other able-bodied working men. Her demeanour changed and she would often put on a mean and tough appearance in order to avoid being bullied and taken advantage of by others.

Life would be much better if the hardship just stopped there, but…

The girl had grown up like a strand of wild hay; no one cared for or taught her things, not even the very basics of femininity. And this naïvety pushed her to the bottom of despair when she was tricked into giving her virginity to a porter, not knowing the things to come.

The day she started to notice her weight changing was also the day she lost contact with the porter, leaving her frightened and with no one to turn to. With nothing to hide her growing belly, she soon became the topic of gossip. The trip to the market each morning grew harder and harder. Many times, she had to hold her breath to suppress the physical pain and aches. But even more unbearable was the shame she felt, the shame that forced her to finally leave.

That was the beginning of her sorrowful and lonesome days. The one she had hoped to rely on was long gone and the path ahead looked bleak and hopeless. No longer able to return to the market, she instead turned to weaving baskets to make a living. Every night in her little shack, as tears streamed down her face and through the threads in her hands, she wondered why life had to be so harsh.

Is it true that life is an endless series of difficult events? Looking back on her past, she couldn't find a single happy day, only a broken fate. Now, to make things worse, she had to worry about the baby growing inside her each day. Desperate and helpless, all she could do was cry out to a Higher Being she wasn't even sure existed.

The unexpected but inevitable day eventually arrived. Struggling to get by without any relatives, experience, money, or even the basic necessities for childbirth, she had to beg for assistance all the way through the whole ordeal, and her little child made his first cry bathed in the tears of his mother.

Day after day, misery and poverty clung to her. No matter how hard she tried, she could never make enough to raise her child. Her vision was getting blurry, food was always scarce, and even requests to borrow a broom from her neighbours were met with disdainful looks. In the midst of her despair, she longed for a day when she could escape her current life, when she would no longer be alone and there would be someone to share and go through life with her.

Her longing appeared to be fulfilled when she met an honest-looking man who expressed feelings for her. She agreed to live together with him in hopes of having someone to lean on. But contrary to what she had thought, things continued to get worse after she gave birth to another two children. Her life had become caught up in a perpetual cycle of hunger, poverty, sickness, and debt no matter how much she struggled. Her husband was unemployed and the whole family relied on her small sandwich stall to survive. Often, she would have to stay up till three in the morning just to sell some bread to pay her debts. She sent her children to school without money to pay for their tuition, and the children would regularly witness their parents being cursed at and harassed by debt collectors. On days when the children fell ill, she would bring them to the hospital without a single cent in her pocket, begging for leftover food for them and waiting for them to get better before sneaking them out.

As time passed, the family's debt continued to pile up, leaving them in suffering, as if under an inescapable curse. She wondered why she had to live like a beggar when she hadn't committed any bad deed in life. It broke her heart to hear her own daughter asking to be sold to Taiwan or Japan for some money to save the family. Even then, that plan failed — she had brought her daughter to the buyer, but her daughter was rejected because she was too young. On the long walk back home, she continued to be conflicted by the disappointment of not having any money and the joy of not losing a child. The mixed emotions built up in her chest and left her feeling like she was going to explode. She just wanted to shout out to the Higher Being, "Would death be the end of this?" She had thought about death many times, and now the idea was becoming stronger than ever.

However, she experienced a divine encounter which she only managed to recognise long after…

One afternoon while she was lost in a jumble of thoughts, an aunt of hers stopped by and brought her to church. In the midst of all her worries, she sat down, listened to people praising God and thought to herself, "I'm as good as dead, how can I sing?" And then it struck her that God was the Higher Being she had been crying out to all these years. That night, she bowed her head and invited God into her life, marking the beginning of a dramatic turnaround.

The following day, a random stranger from her neighbourhood brought her 300,000 Dong to buy gifts for her children so they could celebrate the upcoming Lunar New Year. Holding the money in her hands, she trembled and thought to herself, "God is so amazing!" Never before in her life had she such an amount of money, but more significantly, never before had she entertained the hope that her life would improve. Instead of crying out to a vague Higher Being, she now prayed to God for help and intervention in her life, particularly with the gangsters who would harass her every day to repay the debts she owed. And the things God did amazed her; there seemed to be a divine hand at work. Soon, not only did thugs no longer harass her, but even the harsh letters from the local authority asking her to repay her debts stopped coming. Surely tens of debtors letting her slide could not be a coincidence. From then on, she genuinely sought God out and found the amazing truth of "how He loves her so". Although there were debts that still needed to be paid, she was overcome by an immense peace.

The closer she got to God, the more she realised that her quality of life had improved in extraordinary ways one could never explain. One day, her husband came home and told her he had met an old friend who promised to lend him a motorcycle so he could ferry people for a fee. This encounter was a dream come true for them because they had longed for such an opportunity but never had enough money to rent a motorcycle. Now, her husband had a job and they could send the children to school without having to worry about affording the tuition fees. Her eldest daughter managed to find a job and was helping the family, too. She was overwhelmed by the grace of God and extremely grateful to Him for restoring her eyesight after spending a period of time praying and fasting (her eyesight had diminished in earlier years as a result of her constant crying and overworking at night under dim light).

Sitting next to me now, she wipes her tears and says, "God loves me very much! He has made up for all my days of hardship in such amazing ways. Within less than a year, He has transformed my life." She continues telling me about the blessings she experienced through the marriage between her eldest daughter and a Vietnamese American. Her second daughter married a Christian minister, and her two little daughters are very well behaved even though they are growing up in a bad community (her own brothers had joined a gang, working as pimps at brothels and becoming addicted to drugs). It's certainly clear that God not only brought her out of her dark and harsh life, but also continues to cover her family in the light of His protection.

Today, she is no longer indebted to anyone but she joyfully acknowledges her debt of love to the people around her.

Holding her hand, I thanked God for giving me this opportunity to know such a special individual. I realised that God had a plan when He placed her in such difficult life situations, and it is no surprise to see her becoming a comfort to many who are going through tough times. Just as Paul said in 2 Corinthians 1:4, "[God] comforts us in all our troubles, so that we can comfort those in any trouble with the comfort we ourselves receive from God."

Because of her life's testimony, all the relatives on both her and her husband's sides came to know God. From being a poor, illiterate girl, she eventually found God and dedicated her life to Him and today has become a minister of God's Word to more than fifty people in District 7 (some of whom are more educated than her). She is also a very effective intercessor and prayer warrior.

She smiles as she reads me her favourite Bible verse, Psalm 40:2, "He lifted me out of the slimy pit, out of the mud and mire; He set my feet on a rock and gave me a firm place to stand."

Praise be to God. For more than two thousand years, He has continued to work through the lives of many simple people who give themselves to Him.

I was so happy,
I got out of bed and tried to stand on my
feet. I could stand!

I am Healed

Cao Nguyen, based on the testimony of Khanh Thi H.

I am a single mum of six children, five girls and a boy. Since the day my husband passed away our family has been living in extreme poverty in the Ha Tay area in North Vietnam. My husband passed away when my son was only six, and he is now eleven. I have been suffering from sciatica, which causes me excruciating pain when I walk, and a few years ago, I was diagnosed with a leprosy-like disease. My health grew worse, till I was no longer able to go to work and support my family. My older children, who had shouldered many of the responsibilities at home, now had to do my share of work in the planting field. My oldest daughter was 18 at that time.

I soon started to notice cracks on my heel, and they grew larger each day, eventually forming two deep holes. I was in unbearable pain, and the holes grew so big that they could fit an egg inside. I could no longer walk or do anything except crawl and cry out in pain. Although I was taken to many different doctors and hospitals, there was no cure. They could only advise me to take painkillers.

About a year ago, my brother-in-law started to share with me about Jesus. I scoffed and told him not to follow such a strange religion, because no one in the whole village had ever heard of it or followed it. He didn't continue further but told me that I would be healed if I believed in Jesus. I did not believe because I thought I was dying from my disease.

I figured that if the doctors were not able to cure me then no one else could. At that moment, Jesus meant nothing to me. What I really needed was money, food, and many other things, and the Jesus I was told about seemed so far away and unrealistic.

One Sunday, my son went with my brother-in-law to a place called church. He came back and told me that he saw the pastor pray as he laid hands on people, and some of them were healed. So he went to the pastor and asked, "Could you heal my mum? She's also sick."

"Of course! God will heal her if she truly believes in Him. Just bring her here."

"But my mum cannot walk; she is very sick and only able to crawl."

And the pastor replied briefly, "If so, you should believe and accept Jesus as the Lord and Saviour of your life. Then you can lay hands on her and God will heal her."

My son quickly kneeled and prayed to Jesus, and then he ran home to me without waiting for any further instructions from the minister.

"Mummy, I accepted Jesus into my life, I am His son now. I'm going to lay hands and pray for you as the pastor did. I've seen him heal people. Some of them even testified that they thought they were going to die, but now they are healed by God."

"Okay, it's up to you. You can pray for me if you want. I don't know how much time I have left to live."

And so my little son laid his hand on my shoulder. I saw him close his eyes and say, "Jesus, I heard many talk about You as a powerful healer; please have mercy on my mum and heal her!"

Early the next morning, as usual I picked up my hand fan and started flapping at the two big holes on my heels to shoo away the gnats. I had to do it daily as my wound was infected and discharged pus. The odour was unbearable to whoever came close to me — even I could not stand the smell. However, gnats were attracted by the odour and constantly tried to land on it.

But today I was surprised to see no gnats around. I realised that the bleeding and discharge had stopped. I was so happy, I got out of bed and tried to stand on my feet. I could stand! I started crying and shouting for joy. It had been a very long time since I had last been able to stand. I took some tentative steps and was thrilled that I could actually walk. My children were woken by my shouts of joy. My youngest son ran in with my daughters. None of them understood what was going on; we just hugged each other and cried for joy like never before.

Soon after, I went all around the village to show them that I now could walk. Wherever I went, I told people about the one called Jesus who had healed me. There was no one in my village who did not know about my near-death condition, and everyone rejoiced with me. They asked me to show them my feet. The two deep holes were still there, but the miracle was that I no longer felt any pain, and the bleeding and discharge had also stopped.

All my relatives were very happy to hear about my healing, and that I can still live to take care of my children. If I were to die, who would be able to raise my six children?

I started to go to church and the whole church was very glad to hear my testimony. I found out that many, like me, had also been healed from various chronic diseases. I started to study God's Word. A leader suggested that since I now belong to God, I should invite Him to be the Master of my life and my household. And I should only worship Him alone.

I gladly followed God's teaching and got rid of all the old statues and idols that I used to worship. However, the villagers around me started to persecute me for my faith. They were happy that I had been healed but at the same time angry because I no longer worshipped and gave offerings to their gods as before. No matter how hard I tried to explain, they still didn't understand.

Perhaps many people are still having doubts about my God, but I don't. I have experienced so powerfully His physical healing and His saving grace in my life.

Each day, He not only eased my pain but also healed me by regenerating new muscles in my heels. At the time that I am writing this testimony, I have been healed for five months. Today, the two holes are still quite deep, and some people are even afraid to look at them. But I know clearly that God is still healing me amazingly. Now I cannot fit an egg in the holes but maybe a small mandarin (*kumquat*). Praise be to God!

Who has ever cried every night
because of their children?
Who has ever felt the pain of seeing
their children consumed by an
addiction to drugs?

Returning from Darkness

Based on the testimony of Diem and her son,
Duc-Trung

Raised in a family belonging to the communist party, Diem grew up learning the value of hard work and self-sacrifice. As a loyal wife and mother, she spent many years working hard overseas to establish a comfortable life for her husband and children. However, her return home was the beginning of unexpected and unbearable heartache; she discovered that two of her sons, in whom she had placed her hope and pride, were now drug addicts.

During that difficult time, she fought with all her might to make sure her children finished school, even going to the unimaginable extent of ensuring they had sufficient doses of drugs so that they would not be tired or get cravings while at school. She can never forget the days of braving the hostile weather to wait outside the school gate in an attempt to keep her children away from bad influences, only to realise that her efforts did not improve anything. Slowly but surely, drugs were dragging her sons to the brink of death.

Duc-Trung, the eldest son, knew that he belonged to a family with good academic heritage. While speaking of his father, an engineer, and his mother, an inventory officer, there seemed to be a great sense of pride in his voice. But Trung almost let everything go to waste.

By the time he became a teenager, life's routine had become boring for Trung. His desire to feel manly and seek thrills soon led him into a life of crime. How cool it would be to steal something and get chased by people, he thought. Unfortunately, the gap between a thought and an action, for Trung, was very small and easily bridged.

All those days while his parents were busy with work, Trung would occupy himself in the company of his friends. Sometimes they would pick fights with random people, other times they would shoplift. When even these were not enough to satisfy them, gambling became an attractive form of entertainment. Trung lived each day without any feelings of regret or uneasiness.

When the "Narcotic Storm" hit North Vietnam, Trung and many of his peers were willing victims, drawn to it with too much curiosity and not enough understanding. Trung recalled, "Even though we knew drugs were bad, we could not foresee their destructive effects. We told each other that whatever people forbade us to do, whatever people condemned, we wanted to try even more."

It was this attitude that started Trung on the road to addiction. As each day, month, and year went by, whatever beautiful dream or blissful ambition that Trung had slowly perished. Instead, every thought that went through his mind revolved around how to get another fix of drugs to feed his craving. The door to the future became so far and unreal that, as far as he was concerned, it was essentially closed.

Being the determined woman that she is, Diem sought all possible solutions as she tried to untangle her sons from this despairing situation. Not only did she consult modern doctors for advice, but she even travelled as far as Yen Bai and Lang Son to get spiritual help from well-known healers. In her desperation, she sold her stocks and donated her earnings to the temple in the hope that things would improve, but all her efforts were ultimately in vain.

Time heals people but it can also erode them, even the strong ones like Diem. Her family's possessions were gradually sold one by one until nothing valuable was left. Not even the eating bowls were spared; her sons sold them in exchange for drugs.

Diem was so desperate and singularly focused on stopping her sons' addiction that she quit her job. After a long time of trying and failing, she eventually had to lock her sons up in their room and took responsibility for bringing them food and taking care of their hygiene. When they were sober, she would take the opportunity to give them advice but when their cravings hit, she could only lock herself out and sit quietly in grief.

Some people use the saying "two yokes on one neck" to describe a burden. For Diem, having to carry just two yokes would have been considered a blessing. Ever since she began tending to her children's addiction, she lost the strength and energy needed to take care of her husband and her youngest son, also a teenager. Her life descended in a vicious spiral; her relationship with her husband started to deteriorate and her youngest son constantly ran away from home.

Many nights, she sat alone in the dark feeling completely defeated. Tears fell, and she asked herself why, if her parents were good people and she hadn't done anything wrong, did she have to endure such pain in life?

Although Trung and his brother both loved their mother dearly, they were unable to resist the addictive power of drugs. The cravings sometimes caused such restlessness and unbearable pain that Trung and his mother had to walk around the streets at 3 a.m. in the cutting cold of Hanoi just to buy drugs.

How could he be so ignorant of the tears running down his mother's weary face? Feeling troubled and crushed, he had promised his mother dozens of times that he would give up drugs and seek help, but he was still powerless to do so.

His struggle with addiction, along with the experiences of his peers, led Trung to believe life was hopeless. Some friends who had been pitching in money with him to buy drugs one night were found dead the next morning in a street corner. Another died and was dragged out of a public restroom by his own parents. Worse still were some others who lived under the death sentence of AIDS. The luckier ones ended up in prison. Many of his friends were very young but he never saw them again. The weight of his own helplessness caused Trung to bow his head and realise that he too would soon be visited by inescapable doom.

Amidst the jumble of her clattering thoughts, Diem suddenly remembered an old friend whose child was also an addict. As they had not seen each other for a long time, Diem called her with the intention of finding out whether her son was still alive. To her surprise, Diem was greeted by a happy voice asking, "Is that you, Diem? How are your two sons?"

"They…are still the same," Diem replied hesitantly.

"If so, come visit me, okay?" For some reason, this casual invitation filled Diem's heart with a great hope.

"When can I come?" she asked eagerly.

"I'll see you on Thursday night." Her tone of voice seemed so peaceful, not at all what Diem was expecting from someone whose son was a drug addict.

In a divine arrangement, Dung, Diem's youngest son who had just returned after running away from home was the one who took her to see that friend. It turned out that Diem was not the only one visiting her friend; she had been invited to a gathering of many mothers whose children were also drug addicts.

In the first hour Diem heard stories from others testifying to God's love and His blessings. Some were mothers whose children had been drug-free for months, while others had been drug-free for years. Only Diem still had sons who were under the influence of drugs. This must be the place for me, her heart cried out. Here she could freely share her burdens and find sympathy and comfort. But more than anything, here she found a place of hope for her two addicted sons.

That night, Diem and her youngest son accepted Christ. Before, Diem used to worship and bow down to idols. But after accepting Christ, she instead prayed and lifted up her problems to Him and found a huge and immediate difference. She was filled with a sense of peace that she had never experienced before in her life. Her faith continued to grow each day like "a tree planted by streams of water" and she shared about God with her sons.

Eventually, Trung was brought to the church his mother often talked about. This church was also the very place where the lives of many of his addict friends were changed. The environment of the church was a very intimate and loving one, such that Trung had not encountered for a long time. As an addict, people would usually try to avoid contact with him wherever he went. In church, however, many came to talk to him, while others would greet him with a friendly look, a smile, or a clap on the shoulder. Trung was captivated by the warmth and sincerity he had found.

After that visit, Trung found in himself a burning desire to rise above his addiction. For the first time in many years, something awoke in him. The wish to escape his dark life had never been so strong. Looking at some of his friends who'd broken free from the bondage of drugs, Trung craved to experience just a glimpse of that. He lifted his request to God who, hearing the voice of Trung's sincere heart, didn't just give what he asked for but exceeded it.

Demolishing an old house to build a new one is not an easy task. Similarly, renewing a person's life cannot be done in a matter of days. But God did it in Trung's life gently, simply, and miraculously. After one year of learning about God, isolated from evil influences, Trung continued his studies and finished college. He didn't have to think hard about the direction of his future because he had decided to offer himself to be a living witness for God. Trung told his friends about God, using his life testimony, and through that many were drawn to Him.

Trung is now married to a God-fearing woman and they are getting ready to have their second son. He is also helping out in a church called Ezekiel, guiding many young people whose lives would have had no hope without God.

Smiling with joy, Diem says, "God had great mercy on my family. Praise be to Him because He brought us out of extremely dark days! Every time I think of it now, it feels like I'm living in a dream."

Before, people tied me with rope, restraining my insanity with medication. Today, God has untied me and He comforts me with His love.

He Never Lets Me Go

Phuong Thi Phan

I grew up in a less fortunate environment. My family was poor and broken, and at the age of fifteen I had to stop school in order to make a living by sewing market goods. Life became harder when my mother decided to enter a second marriage with another man, eventually giving birth to his child. I was dismayed and lonely because of the lack of love from both my parents.

Life went on drearily; love was a luxury that I could only hope for but never get. However, my heart kept yearning for it. When I was eighteen, I came to know and fall in love with a young man. Because of the lack of love in my own childhood, I came to love him wholeheartedly but my feelings were not reciprocated. This unrequited love made me suffer, and I started to build up a hatred toward life. I hated the situation I was trapped in and wanted to escape. My mind would constantly dwell on the thought of making a lot of money so I could change my life.

The year was 1967. The war was going on, and there were a lot of American soldiers in Vietnam. I was introduced to a *tai pan* — a club manager — who took me in, prepared me, and sent me to learn how to dance. Each night I would follow her to the club and assist in providing "guest services". However, after the Mau Than insurrection, all the clubs were closed down and I was sent to Cam Ranh. At this place where many American soldiers were encamped, I found the opportunity to make money. That was the sole purpose of my life: taking on any job that could earn a lot of money, regardless of what it entailed.

Before I turned 20, I let my lust for money turn me into an object of lust for many American soldiers. Although most of them just took advantage of my body, some came to love me and wanted to bring me to America to settle down. I always rejected their offers because I did not have feelings for any of them. Soon after I had begun this vicious cycle of life, I became pregnant with the child of an American Air Force major. By this time, the American soldiers were starting to get driven out of Vietnam. Faced with the prospect of carrying such a burden without the father around, I chose to abort my child. I committed the very horrific act of killing my own baby when it was almost full-term.

To make use of my remaining youth, I moved back to Saigon, hooking up with people of wealth and status to serve as their mistress. Even though I made a lot of money, I always felt lonely. My ears heard many loving words but I could not find anyone who truly loved me. My youth continued to drift away.

After 30 April 1975, the country attained total liberation. I lived with a married man who later became the father of my daughter. He was one of the people who organised illegal escapes by boat, and I managed to keep a considerable amount of the gold that he earned. This lavish lifestyle did not last for long; one of the escapes did not go according to plan, and the man was arrested. The police searched our home and uncovered a very large stash of gold.

At the age of 28, my life took on a new turn. One month after giving birth to my daughter, I had to hide from the police because of my involvement with her father and what he'd done. After two years of living in fear, I was finally arrested and imprisoned for a year. I never managed to contact my daughter's father again after I was released.

My freedom from jail marked the beginning of many difficult years as I hopped from job to job, trying to provide for my daughter and myself. I was unable to hold down a steady job for long, and eventually had to sell my home and move to a smaller residence in order to have enough money to try out new business endeavours. But the more I tried, the more money I lost. Although I worked to the point of exhaustion each day, my nights were spent tossing and turning restlessly as I was haunted by my past and worried about the uncertain future. Things took such a toll that in 1995 I suffered a mental breakdown. I was prone to fits of madness, in which I would lose control of my sanity and walk around in the rain without any clothes on.

My daughter had to grow up in a miserable environment. Her father was missing, her mother was mentally ill, and financial difficulty cast a permanent shadow over her. Every year, she had to take me to Cho Quan Mental Hospital so I could get treated for my illness. The treatment did not seem to be effective and I often had to be tied down when I lost control of myself.

In 1997, my daughter was offered a job at a hair salon. The owner is a Christian and she led my daughter to Christ. The pastor and people from the church came to my home to pray for me but, instead of accepting God, I continued to allow the darkness to drown me. My mental condition deteriorated each day. To make things worse, I had hyperthyroidism, which caused my hands to shake and eyes to protrude, making me look terrifying. I felt so hopeless and discontented with life that I overdosed on sleeping medication in an attempt to commit suicide. For some reason, I did not die. I slept for three days in a row before waking up, feeling totally exhausted.

My life continued to feel sad and meaningless. Each wearisome day was full of worries and all I wanted was death. Even then, death didn't come easily. On one occasion, I used a razor to slit my wrist (the scar remains till this day), causing me to bleed all over my bed. I was afraid people would find out what had happened to me, so I snuck out to the park and sat there till midnight but I still did not die. It was only later that I realised this was an act of God's mercy, part of His plan to rescue me.

Our small house next to the Cau Kieu channel was confiscated in 1999. It was only in such a time of need that I began to truly understand the fickleness of life. I reached out for help from anyone I knew, whether they were mere acquaintances or friends for many years. Everyone was cold and indifferent to my plight. Given how unhappy I was with my own life and how upset I was with people, my heart was full of anger and hatred.

One day, I found myself in front of my daughter's Bible. I picked it up and opened it. I read about God's love, which seemed like such an amazing thing that I could never imagine experiencing it in this life. With great curiosity and very little understanding, I went to look for Ms Van, the lady who had led my daughter to Christ. Ms Van brought me to church to let me hear about God, and around Christmas of 1999 I opened my heart to accept Christ.

Like the prodigal son returning to his father's home, my life started to change. How could I ever thank God enough? I continued to learn about Him through Bible studies and I witnessed His wonderful transforming power that turned me from a person living in guilt to a daughter of the Most High God. He changed the selfish person that I was and taught me how to share with others. I was insecure and hopeless, but He filled me with His peace and showered me with His blessings.

Over the past ten years, I have continued to be renewed each day by the power of God's goodness. Before, people tied me with rope, restraining my insanity with medication. Today, God has untied me and He comforts me with His love. I recently had a chance to visit my old neighborhood, and people were no longer able to recognise the crazy woman from Cau Kieu.

Thank God for healing my hyperthyroidism ever since I prayed and decided to rely on Him instead of my daily medication. My eyes no longer bulge out as before, and God gives me the strength to climb up and down the four levels of stairs in my apartment building each day so I can help cook for my children and grandchildren. I'm very grateful for all that He has done for me.

This year's Christmas marks my eleventh year of walking with God. I always like to talk about my God. He is amazingly wonderful. I can't imagine what life would be like if I had not met Jesus. I also owe much to those who guided and helped me know Him. These people are examples for me to follow as I continue to bring others to Him. Today, my brother and sister-in-law have received Christ and are also walking with Him faithfully. I even had the opportunity to witness to my neighbours and lead two of them to God. I really wish that many people will be saved from this corrupted world and experience God's amazing love like I have.

All the beauty and money I used to possess did not bring me joy and happiness. Although I am poor today, I have never been happier in my life. Praise God!

The fire of her
candle went out.
But she never
knew that from
her candle, mine
was lit.

Lighting the Candle
Cuong Manh Le

I grew up in a wealthy family. I was used to indulgence and had many more acquaintances than true friends. Although it would not be accurate to call me a spoiled son, it would be worse to consider me an exemplary one. I learned to smoke at the age of fourteen, and after two years cigarettes had become my inseparable companions. Despite knowing the adverse effects of smoking, I still could not quit.

My parents had a small sandal manufacturing company in a suburban area. During their free time, the air would be filled with the workers' chatter. Some would complain about money, some would gossip about others. When there was nothing left to talk about, they would discuss the weather. Of all the conversations, though, I found none to be more hilarious or silly than the stories coming from Mr Thiem's fifteen-year-old daughter.

All day long she wouldn't stop talking about God's blessings upon her family. One day, she mentioned how God healed the family's buffalo. A couple of days later, she eagerly talked about His blessing on her school of fish. The story was so ridiculous that I could barely contain my laughter. She was never ashamed to share her stories, and every time something new happened, she would enthusiastically go on and on about it ("…yesterday, God healed our chicken!"). I saw in her eyes something very simple but vehement. At first, all her stories merely amused me but, after a period of time, I started to grow in curiosity and interest.

One day after many years, my companionship with cigarettes started to pay its dues. I developed chest pains and breathing problems that severely weakened and exhausted me. During one fit of pain, the testimonies of the girl rang in my head: "God healed our buffalo…He blessed our school of fish…" It became a hope in me and I prayed, "God, if You are real, please help me quit smoking."

Amazingly, after that occasion, I could no longer smoke. Every time I sensed the smell of cigarette smoke, I would feel extremely nauseous. I knew then that I had been completely freed from the invisible bondage that had taken hold of me for so many years. I have spent a lot of time thinking back on this wonderful miracle.

About a month later, the girl was on her way home to get ready for church. She was carefree as usual, not knowing it would be her last time walking on that familiar road. A motorcycle steered by a drunk rider collided with her and she died. I was speechless as I looked at the girl, once so full of life and conviction, now lying on a gurney under a white sheet.

Her funeral was the most special one I had ever attended. There were no drums or trumpets, no incense, no agonising, mournful cries. There were only sad tears, but in the sadness I saw a strange resolve that was difficult to explain — a powerful sense of hope in something much greater. In that moment I realised: after death, there is still eternal life.

There are many ways to start a new life in faith. For me, it was at that funeral where I bowed my head to confess, "Lord! I want to experience this kind of eternal life."

The fire of her candle had gone out. But she never knew that from her candle, mine was lit.

She lived her life without a single happy day, seeing her youth, wealth, and strength slipping away. She was only left with a body that was shrivelling up, weighed down by all kinds of burdens.

Last Farewell to Darkness

D.T., based on the testimony of Le Thi-The

There was a sound of footsteps up the stairs. A young face with fair skin and wavy hair greeted me with a smile. I tried to recall that familiar face, and I finally uttered with amazement, "Oh, wow! Is that you, The? Wow! I cannot believe this…"

I was so happy and surprised that I didn't know what else to say except the word "wow".

Although I had not met The for just four years, the encounter was a huge surprise.

I still remember that first day she accepted Christ. She had just passed through a big storm in life. She was scrawny, and stood an arm's length away from me. Tears rolled down her weathered face as she sobbed out her life story, letting her tears flow down her chin and neck and soak through her dark-coloured shirt. I can never forget that image.

That very same woman was sitting in front of me, so refreshed and full of life.

I wondered, "How could she have changed so much?"

Tying her wavy hair to the back, she started to tell me about her life:

The was born and grew up in the Ma Tay area of Hanoi, Vietnam's capital. Her family was pretty well off because her mum was a drug dealer. Tapping on the mattress she was sitting on, she said, "Back then I used to sleep on money, not on a mattress like this."

She had married at seventeen, and had things that many married couples would have had to save up for years to get: a home, a car, and assets. Life for her seemed so easy. However, happiness was something so far away. It was soon clear to her that money could not buy happiness. The newlyweds went through a difficult time of conflicts, and six months later, her husband was arrested due to a fight with the in-laws. She gave birth to her first son without knowing what love is.

She made a living as a voodoo practitioner, being called "Keke Cong Khanh", meaning that her family had been passing down the voodoo tradition, from her great-great-grandmother to her generation. She calculated and said, "My family has 'served' for seven generations." (It dawned on me then why I had felt a chill when I met her for the first time. I had sensed some kind of unexplainable, strange darkness imprinted on her eyes, lips, and body.)

I asked her curiously, "I've only heard the term 'going into a trance', but I don't really know what it is. Could you tell me more about it?"

She chuckled and said, "This is how you would sit, and you would have a big red scarf as a head covering. There are 36 prices (level of spirits) and each goes in accordance with its own covering." Looking deep into the space in front of her, she recalled the vague memories of when she used to be the head voodoo practitioner. Other practitioners typically do four trances a year (at the beginning and end of the year, and at the beginning and end of summer). But she was different — she used to have so many customers that she lost count of them. People sought her to heal illnesses, to find lost possessions, for building advice, for marital fortune, and even for relationship issues. She had to go into a trance for all sorts of answers. She was known as the "capital voodoo master" because it was usual for her to perform trance sessions for millions of Vietnamese Dollars.

Yet she was always suffering. The career of fortune telling, spirit calling, and soul catching has its own set of problems. Besides, the money would go just as fast as it came. She remembered how she was often bitter, "My husband and son could not enjoy a good meal, I didn't even have nice clothes, and my family was a mess." Trances also involved running around and jumping, after which there would be a deep spiritual and physical tiredness.

Each time the dark world came crashing in, she became a slave who had to pour out offering money in exchange for prosperity. But after a couple of months, everything would go back to normal. And again she would have to continue with her offering and worship. There was not a day of peace to relax. Moreover, the power of darkness made her meaner and more cruel as she kept on living in that world. In those days, everyone — from her family to the neighbours — was afraid of her. She once slashed her husband, cutting through three thick layers of his clothing. At another time, she kicked her son so hard that he bumped his head against the wall and bled. Even when the authorities intervened, she tore up their pants and cried out loud in public.

Darkness had such a powerful dominion over her. She lived her life without a single happy day, seeing her youth, wealth, and strength slipping away. She was only left with a body that was shrivelling up, weighed down by all kinds of burdens. She soon had to open a small stall selling rice noodles to provide for her family. Many times she wondered why life had become so tough. She did voodoo to help people with their love lives, but her husband was having an affair with someone else. She did voodoo to help people find peace while her son was suffering in a rehabilitation centre. She did voodoo to cure others, but no one could heal her own illness. She was desperate.

One day, a woman with a small stature and a kind face came to eat at her stall. She started up a conversation in her South Vietnamese accent and talked to The about God. At first The didn't like it but listened out of courtesy. Soon she ran out of patience and said to the lady, "Actually, I'm a voodoo practitioner, and it's been my family's tradition." With pride, she thought to herself, "My family has been doing this for seven generations; why would I want to listen about God from this strange Southern woman?" But to be courteous, she reached out her hand and received a small book and a Bible from the woman.

As each day passed, her family's burden continued to weigh heavily on her shoulders. Besides her drug-addicted sons, she had to take care of her father, a brother and sister in jail, her nephews and nieces, as well as her sisters-in-law. With her noodle stall, she had to make enough money to feed ten mouths at home.

But there was nothing worse than the day she heard the news that her two sons in rehab were diagnosed with HIV. That day, walking under the pouring rain, she cried out, "O God of heaven and earth! If there's Someone who can save my children, I will worship you till the day I die!"

That night, her heart filled with sadness and heaviness, she remembered the words from the Southern woman. She took out the Bible, started reading it and thought to herself, "This is my last hope." Her husband recalled, "In that book, there is a story of a man who was dead for four days and Jesus brought him back to life!"

After thinking for a moment, he asked The, "Where is the Southern woman's number, let's call her so she can pray for our kids!" (He used to work in Poland and had heard about God there.)

Like a drowning person who sees a float, she immediately looked for the number and called the woman. It was 11 p.m. Then the waiting started.

One night she was sitting down reading her Bible. While she was concentrating on the words, it seemed like there was a hand removing a veil from her face, although she was not wearing any veil, and a light shone onto the pages of her Bible. It was so bright that she didn't even need to use her reading glasses. She knew there was something very strange happening around her. Turning each page attentively, she reached Deuteronomy 18:10–12: "Let no one be found among you who sacrifices their son or daughter in the fire, who practices divination or sorcery, interprets omens, engages in witchcraft, or casts spells, or who is a medium or spiritist or who consults the dead. Anyone who does these things is detestable to the Lord; because of these same detestable practices the Lord your God will drive out those nations before you."

She was silent. Fear started to set in. She quickly closed her Bible, but those words continued to echo in her head like a death sentence. She longed for the day that she could meet the woman who had told her about God.

That day soon came. Even though the meeting was at five in the afternoon, she closed her stall at 3.30 p.m., and sat and waited with her husband and son.

It was on 11 August 2005 that she made her decision to accept Christ. It was the day that the stubborn, callous, and hardened person in her was broken; the day that she knew eternal damnation was no longer her sentence. The tears that had long dried were now falling rapidly when she heard the woman's simple but sincere prayers. She could feel the love of God and the deep care from that stranger. No one had ever shown love to her in such a manner.

Since the day she accepted Christ, she found comfort and warmth every time she gathered with other believers in the church. She used to put her name and her son's name into her favorite verses of the Bible. Although she did not have much knowledge about God at that time, she had strong faith in Him. She started to pray for her loved ones, hoping that they will one day come to God.

Not too long after, the rehab centre called her to send her son home because he was in a critical condition and waiting to die. She brought him home and asked people from church to pray for him to receive Jesus. Then she brought him back to the centre, but everyone knew that there wasn't much left to do for HIV patients at the last stage. The next day, the hospital sent him back again. Brokenhearted, she was left looking at her son on his deathbed, withered like a corpse, no longer able to eat or take IV. He curled up grimacing with every cough. Everyone in the family went to buy wrapping linen and even prepared a burial place for him, ready for his funeral. However, with the heart of a mother, she prayed to God in tears, "Jehovah! Please give my son just a drop of life!"

That night, she knew that life was leaving her son's body as he lay unconscious. His breath was weak and his body was cold. The woman who brought her to faith came immediately upon hearing about her son's condition. She laid her hand on his forehead and prayed for him. Sitting next to his cold body from dusk to midnight, she supplicated earnestly for him. That went on for quite some time, and his body began to get warmer. Sweat started to run down from his forehead as a sign of life.

At midnight, when The was downstairs, she heard her son calling out with a loud voice, "Mum! Mummy!" She felt puzzled because she thought he was going to die at that moment. She rushed upstairs and was shocked to see him sitting up in bed. She was filled with joy and awe as he said, "Is there anything to eat, mum? I'm so hungry!"

To everyone's amazement her son Long, who had only been taking liquids for months and was almost at the point of death, was sitting up and eating a big bowl of rice, as though to make up for all his time in bed. After he finished, he stood up to clean up the table and then went to wash up all by himself. She stood there looking at him, she could not say anything else besides mumbling, "Oh…That's so strange, thank God! He is so great!"

Since that day, her son has been called "Lazarus" by his friends at church. The "drop of life" that she had asked God for her son that night was granted. Instead of passing away that night, her son lived on for more than two and a half years (from 12 December 2005 to 6 June 2008). He was able to learn about God at the Christian Salvation Centre and be a witness to many other drug addicts. She really had a wonderful time with her son.

The day she sent her son back to God, her heart was filled with peace even though she was sad. She put her faith solely in Him in order to overcome so many trials in life. During times of serious illness, she experienced God's healing and His provision. He protected her through persecution, and He was her Comforter in times of sorrow. Welling up with tears, she said, "I experienced His goodness each and every day."

With a bright and joyful smile, she told me that since the day she lost her son, God had blessed her with many more children — the young people from church. "They call me mum," she said with her voice full of joy.

Although surrounded by many people in her past life, she had never heard a single word of love. But now she is living happily in love. She is always hungry to learn more about God so she can be more fruitful for Him. She also would not hesitate to share with her voodoo friends from the past, "I used to bow down to the nine skies, but now I can come directly before the God of all". Her resounding laugh is so peaceful and relaxed.

God changed her life so that today she can joyfully testify, "But by the grace of God I am what I am, and his grace to me was not without effect…" (1 Corinthians 15:10).

It is dark outside. I look at her and try to picture the voodoo lady of five years earlier. How could I ever give Him enough praise!

Lying down beside them, Mrs Nam let out a deep sigh. The image of the bag of rat poison that her husband had bought to mix into the porridge pot haunted her.

Marvellous God

Van-Sinh Tran, based on the account of Mrs Hong-Phuc Vo Tran,
Mrs Thi Thi Tran, and the third child of Mr Cong Van Vo

It was a beautiful morning with a clear, blue sky; the flowers were showing off their beauty under the sunlight. Picking up the *Hat Muoi* magazine, I flipped to the contents page, trying to choose an article to read, when I saw this headline, "Writing Contest: Lives that have been changed by God".

"Wow, this is great!" I shouted. I felt all the memories from God's many blessings wash over me and overwhelm my being. Suddenly, I remembered Mr Nam, a man I had met several years earlier…

⁓

In those days, the land of Ca Mau was a remote place, with only streams and rivers. A farmer with his wife and children came all the way from Nha Trang in Central Vietnam to this place, hoping to start a new life. The first days were tough. There were many burdens on his shoulders. Mr Nam had nothing more than the clothes on him and a few duffel bags. Fortunately, he received some help from a relative, who let him and his family stay in a small hut in a corner of their field. They lived like this through rainy days and windy nights. At that time, he and his wife were still healthy and able to plough the field to feed their children. But their happiness was quickly gone when his wife was diagnosed with rheumatism. Her legs hurt — especially her knees — making walking extremely difficult. Their savings soon dried up, and debt began to accumulate.

Looking at his wife and children, Mr Nam's heart was filled with sadness as his family was getting close to the end of the road. Even so, he tried hard to work and find ways to bring his family out of poverty. He endured the hard days and the rough journey with poor food and medication, reciting Buddhist prayers every night. All his hope that one day things would change was in his religion. However, his prayers grew to become an empty sound of endless sorrow.

He had nothing else except a sick wife and a bunch of children. Disappointment, weariness, and despair seemed to go on forever. One day he wondered, "Death?" Only death could offer a way out. He deliberated and considered, before deciding to tell his wife about this idea. After hearing her husband out, Mrs Nam grew quiet, looked at him with pain in her face, and cried. Tears of sorrow flowed down her face. Is life meant to be that short? Did her whole family have to depart from this world like this?

That afternoon, as the children were taking a nap, Mrs Nam watched their pale and innocent faces that looked so gentle in their sleep. Lying down beside them, Mrs Nam let out a deep sigh. The image of the bag of rat poison that her husband had bought that morning to mix into the porridge pot haunted her. She gently touched the faces of her children, the fruit of her womb. Did they have to die? Did their family have to die? She bowed her head in silence. She started to think of ways that death could come as quickly and painlessly as possible. In her muddled thoughts, she suddenly heard a whisper, "Read the Bible! Just read the Bible! Read the Holy Bible."

Her head shot up. Beads of sweat ran down from her brow. Who had whispered "read the Bible" into her ears thrice? It was so strange! She thought about it carefully and decided to keep the matter a secret because she did not know who to share it with.

That evening, Mrs Nam asked her husband to postpone the suicide plan, and to instead get her some medicine the next day. He met Mr Tu Chau, a blind man living in a corner of the village. Mr Nam shared with him about his family's situation. Mr Tu advised, "You and your wife should come to know Christ."

After listening to Mr Tu about the love of Christ, a glimmer of hope was sparked in Mr Nam's heart. He ran home to his wife and told her what he had heard from Mr Tu. Mrs Nam was shocked, and she shared with him about the strange whisper she had heard the day before. They were both speechless.

The next day, they decided to visit Mr Tu so that they could ask more about the Bible. Although Mr Tu is blind, he truly loves God. He faithfully goes to church and studies the Bible diligently. He gladly welcomed Mr and Mrs Nam and explained that the Bible is the Word of God, and the voice Mrs Nam heard was from the Holy Spirit.

After discovering these truths, the couple was very happy. That night they started to read the Bible given by Mr Tu. They felt blessed and the weight on their shoulders seemed to lighten. The more they read, the more they began to understand its contents. When they encountered difficulties, they would consult Mr Tu. They continued to grow in their faith, and their whole family eventually decided to accept Christ. That was around the beginning of 1980.

Since then, Mr Nam's family has experienced the peace of God. They praise God joyfully and no longer think of suicide. God began to work from the inside out — from their hearts to their circumstances. They truly found happiness and joy. I still remember how, because of his love for God's Word, Mr Nam would row his little boat through the night to take his whole family to church in Tan Duc, which is tens of miles away, for Sunday's morning service.

After many years of walking with God, He blessed Mr Nam's family with abundance. They were able to obtain more land to cultivate their crops. They later moved to Hai An Village, where Mr Nam planted rice and harvested shrimps, and God blessed them with a bumper crop. Their living conditions improved greatly. The children were smart and well behaved, excelling in school, and were talented in music and art.

Mr Tu is no longer around. He went up and down rivers and channels to spread the Gospel for more than thirty years, planting countless seeds. From there grew many fellowships and home churches, from Hai An, Vam Dam to the Thay Bay channel, where they continue to thrive and bear fruit.

Today, Mrs Nam lives happily with her children and grandchildren. She still diligently studies God's Word and makes time for ministry. Son, their son, is now the executive pastor of Tan Duc church in Ca Mau. Their youngest daughter and her family are also attending a Ca Mau church. Another daughter married a teacher, and they now go to Tuc Trung church in Dinh Quan, Dong Nai. And that husband is me. I have recorded these memories to paint a beautiful picture of our marvellous God, our just and loving Saviour.

I will forever thank God for His
amazing deliverance…
I have learned a very valuable lesson
about thanksgiving.

The Power of Thanksgiving

"Mummy, when you're out of debt, could you buy me a bag of *si-nack* (snack)?" my six-year-old daughter asked, looking up from a TV commercial.

"Yeah, *si-nack*, okay, Mummy?" her little sister echoed.

Hearing this, tears began to well up in my eyes. I immediately stopped what I was doing and ran over to my daughters. Hugging them tightly, I whispered, "Are you craving for snacks? I will get you some right away. There's no need to wait till then; I can still get you some, my dears."

I will never forget those years of debt, where all the heaviness, worry, and complaints plagued not only myself, but my young daughters as well.

Things fell apart fifteen years ago, when we lived in the old days of real estate fever. Property prices were shooting up every day. Our family's finances were very tight but my husband and I were convinced that investing in property would bring us much profit. We borrowed money from friends, bought some land, and earned the interest that the land yielded as its value increased.

After owning a piece of land for only a short while, its value rose in worth by several gold taels. In his excitement, my husband sold it and invested in a second one. He borrowed even more money so that he could purchase several plots of land at once. While we were still delighting in the quick success we had found, the market suddenly crashed. At first, we thought there wouldn't be a problem, and that the price would soon go up again. People used to say, "Population increases but a square foot doesn't, so no worries." However, for many years in a row, the price not only failed to go up but instead kept dropping. We could not sell the land and had to pay our bank loan every month. Our family began to fall deeper and deeper into debt.

If we had known better, we would have sold everything immediately when we had the chance to. However, we decided to keep holding on to our property and wait for the right time, even as property prices continued to drop. Soon, I began to panic as the problem grew larger and seemingly unending. At first I tried my best to gather money from here and there in an attempt to pay the interest, but after a short time we soon grew exhausted. Looking back now, we realise that everything was in God's control, even in our lack of experience.

Every month, as the due date for the loan repayment loomed over us like a storm cloud, I would wrack my brain, trying to come up with a solution, but I could never find any. Debt was about to crush our lives. To make things worse, our marriage was affected. We did not dare to blame each other but would constantly argue and complain about our situation. I became bitter in my heart because my husband was the one who had eagerly initiated this endeavour. Each day, I could only gather a tiny amount of money for food, barely enough to buy a bundle of vegetables. I was losing weight and no longer cared about eating. My mind was filled only with thoughts of how to get money to repay our debts, send the children to school, and fulfil our daily needs. I was so scared and miserable. I wished to escape from my life and dreamt of going back to my high school years so that I wouldn't have to worry about all these responsibilities.

In our hopelessness, we began to call out to God. Every time I came before Him, I did not even have enough strength to kneel; I could only cast myself down on the ground and cry out to Him. I asked God day and night, "When will I be able to repay all my debts?" But He was silent. He seemed so far away and out of reach.

Things got worse when we entered our third year of debt, as some of our debtors started to ask for their money back. One day, after dropping my children off at school, I went back to my room to pray. My husband was working, and with his back facing me, he said, "I feel so tired and heavy every time I hear your prayers. I think God might be feeling the same way. Shouldn't we be praying differently if we truly believe that everything works out for the good of those who love Him?" I was shocked and annoyed by that comment at first. But a couple of days later, having cooled down and thought about it, I considered that perhaps my husband was right. I had learned in the Bible and shared with others about the power of thanksgiving, and of trusting that God will provide, so why was I behaving the way I did? I decided to change my method of praying and see what would happen.

I began to cling onto His Word in 1 Thessalonians 5:16–18, "Rejoice always, pray continually, give thanks in all circumstances". These are verses that I had memorised when I was young without truly understanding what they meant. As I thought about my situation, I saw that I should give thanks even in my debt. I was like a person groping her way in the dark but was now able to see a ray of light to reach for. Romans 8:28, "And we know that in all things God works for the good of those who love him, who have been called according to his purpose" spoke to me as well. I began to recite this promise out loud. Instead of complaining and grumbling, I thanked

God — not for my trouble, but for His greatness, His grace and mercy, and His sovereignty.

From that day on, I lived by faith and trusted in the faithfulness of God even though it seemed as if He was oblivious to my situation. Every time I talked to my children or friends, I obeyed His Word and praised Him in my circumstances. I also shared with them about our struggles and my faith in His deliverance, and that we were waiting on Him.

Soon, Christmas came. While everybody was busy shopping for gifts, my family had no money. In fact, we were on a list of ten families to be given gifts due to financial difficulty. My faith was truly tested then. However, I was not discouraged and continued to praise God daily, refusing to let my lips speak words of complaint or reproach.

Thank God for His faithfulness. In His timing, He allowed us to sell a piece of land to repay some people. Then He helped us sell a second one to repay more debt. Through His divine intervention, some debtors wrote off our debts. Gradually, He resolved our outstanding issues — not in our own way, but in His perfect way. Today, we are saved from debt and have been blessed with a fairly well-to-do life so that we can help others. I will forever thank Him for His amazing deliverance, especially when I read news about people being thrown into jail because of their large debts.

I have learned a very valuable lesson about thanksgiving: we are to praise God in all circumstances. Just as the prophet Habakkuk said:

> "Though the fig tree does not bud
> and there are no grapes on the vines,
> though the olive crop fails
> and the fields produce no food,

though there are no sheep in the pen
and no cattle in the stalls,
yet I will rejoice in the LORD,
I will be joyful in God my Savior.
The Sovereign LORD is my strength;
he makes my feet like the feet of a deer,
he enables me to tread on the heights."
(Habakkuk 3:17–19)

What He did truly changed my life;
He touched my son's body and let me
experience Him in a new way.

The Way He Touched My Life

Thuy Tinh

My son looked back, smiled at me, and walked through the university's gates. A memory unfolded within my mind of him ten years ago, smiling at me as he entered the gates of his elementary school.

Time passes by so fast that sometimes it astonishes me. I can never forget what had happened ten years ago, and every time I'm reminded of it, I'm filled with excitement and amazement, as if it happened only yesterday.

In those days, I was so preoccupied with my business that it was probably my first priority in life. Although I never skipped church on Sunday, taught my children to walk in His ways as my parents did, kept my daily quiet time, and had semi-regular family prayer time, the attractiveness of this world drew me away from my relationship with God. Sometimes, kneeling before Him, I would find myself with no words to say. There were also times when I would be thinking of my customers while praying. My prayers were repetitive: all I asked was for God to protect me and bless my business with success, grant me good health, keep my children well, give my dad good health, grant happiness to my mum, and let peace be upon my siblings. If there weren't any other requests, I would simply end my prayer with "Amen".

The phrase "please give" was repeated every day in my prayer, and God patiently listened. Not once did I ask for an increase in my understanding of Him. I did not ask for the very thing He wanted to hear from me.

One afternoon when I went to fetch my son from school, the teacher complained to me: "You should go home and scold him for not focusing in class. He kept going in and out of the classroom and distracted everyone."

I was surprised at first, but soon discovered that my son had a urinary tract infection and inflammation. I accumulated a thick pile of prescriptions but my son's illness was still not subdued. A year went by, and I started to get more concerned because of the way it affected his daily activities. At school, the teacher let him sit near the door so that he could leave for the restroom without disrupting the class. His teacher also became very concerned about his condition because he had to constantly run to and from the restroom two to four times every period. Besides that, he had to crawl in and out of the sleeping net every five to ten minutes every night to go to the toilet. I eventually had to put him in diapers.

This persisted for more than two years. Many times I could not hold back my tears when he told me that he didn't want to leave the house because he was afraid there would be no restroom available. One day, he said, "I don't want to join the children's choir anymore. What am I going to do if I need to go in the middle of the performance?" Brokenhearted, I asked God how much longer I needed to see my son in this condition.

I sought out many doctors who were known specialists in urology for help. I will forever remember one of them, Dr Vinh, who gave me a positive impression. According to him, my son's condition was one in a million. He carefully monitored my son, and performed many tests on him. He explained that because my son's case was rare, they had to run special tests that involved equipment that are not normally used for children. I was full of hope. I thought that with a good, kind-hearted doctor and modern equipment, they would surely be able to cure my son. But I continued to go back and forth with more prescriptions to be filled. Even though the doctor tried to the best of his abilities, he could not improve my son's condition. He saw the disappointment in my eyes, but could not deny that "his illness is very rare".

My son went on to third grade, and his condition worsened. I had to change his diapers three to five times every night. His urine had a strong infected smell mixed with the smell of medication. On our clothes drying rack, there were more of his diapers than our whole family's clothes. I was battered by my son's suffering, and I complained to God, "God, what should I do now?" Under much distress, I called my cousin who is also a doctor, and he promised to introduce me to another urologist at Cho Ray Hospital. But unfortunately the doctor was away on a business trip in another country. I had been counting each day, eagerly looking forward to meeting this doctor. However, God had an amazing plan. That night, our family gathered for prayer. I asked everyone to narrate a story in which God had performed a healing.

My husband mentioned the healing of the ten lepers.

My older son talked about Jesus healing the paralytic man.

My sick son told the story of God giving the blind man back his sight.

And my niece read about the healing of the woman with the issue of blood.

Everybody shared briefly, and then I ended with a prayer, "Heavenly Father, we are believing in a God who stays the same yesterday, today, and forever. Would you please heal my son?" I asked with a small glimmer of faith although my heart was full of sadness. It had been three years and my prayer was getting shorter each day.

Our prayer time ended, and as usual, my little son placed his potty beside his bed while I folded the diapers that would be used that night. I asked him, "Do you want God to heal you as He did the blind man, the paralytic man, and the lepers in the Bible?"

He was lying on the bed but sprang up, "Yes, I do!"

"Then you should ask God to heal you now!" I said and continued to fold the diapers.

My son sat up straight and was ready to say his prayer, but the urge to pee hit him again. He said, "Let me go one more time and then I'll pray!"

Looking at him, my heart wrenched. I told him, "You don't need to leave your bed! Because when you ask, God will heal you just as He did for the men in the Bible!"

He squeezed the pillow in his hand, suppressing the urge, and began to pray, "Dear God, I don't want to pee again! Please help me to not have to pee again. Amen!"

His "Amen" sounded like a cheer! He lay down and went to sleep peacefully. I put a diaper on him and gently placed the rest at the corner of the bed.

I was exhausted and also fell asleep quickly. At midnight, I woke up as usual; it was time to change his diaper. In the semi-darkness, I touched him and he was still dry. I thought to myself, "That's strange! It is almost midnight but he still has not peed?"

I turned and looked at the clock. It wasn't midnight — it was already five o'clock! I could even hear some noise from the morning market nearby. It had been three years since I had such a long sleep. Every time my son peed, the wetness would make him twist and turn, and I would have to wake up and change his diaper. But tonight was the first time after so many nights that he slept soundly all the way — and with a dry diaper. How can I explain how I felt at that moment! Looking at the pile of dry diapers on the bed, I started to remember what had happened that night before we went to bed. Trembling, I whispered, "Thank You, God!" as my tears started to fall.

More than ten years have gone by, but I can't stop myself from trembling every time I'm reminded of what God has done. This is not a Bible story of a Jew's healing some two thousand years ago; this is the story of my son's healing today. My son's illness was healed by God completely and immediately after his simple — and even funny — prayer that one night in 2001. It has been more than ten years, but this event is always a fresh and meaningful memory to our family.

Besides God, no one could have done such an extraordinary and amazing thing. He really cared for and did not disregard such an innocent but earnest prayer of an eight year-old boy. He is full of mercy, slow to anger, and compassionate toward this mother with her little faith. What He did truly changed my life; He touched my son's body and let me experience Him in a new way.

Who can wipe away the dark clouds of my life besides God? The joy and peace that I had never experienced didn't just last for a day, a week, or a month. It has lasted for twenty years.

The Lord is My Song

Phuoc Thi Tran

I grew up in a family with many siblings. My mum had passed away early in my life. My growing-up years were tough — the country was changing and there were more suffering people than happy ones, including myself, the most miserable among all. There was always something that worried me; troubles were unstoppable. My eyes said it all. "Why does your sister have such sad eyes?" a friend of my sister once asked when she saw me for the first time.

People in their twenties are usually optimistic and cherish life, but I was different. I was like a person groping in the dark within a cell, trying to find a way out, and finding nothing but disappointment. My mind was full of worries for my family. How could we go on living when we didn't have household registration, and my younger siblings could not even go to school. Our future seemed so messed up and the only way out I could think of was crossing the border, which was dangerous.

In order to find some peace for my soul, I often went to the temple after work and hoped that the quietness would calm the raging storm of turmoil in me. I carried water, buffed the jars, collected wood and dried them, and swept up the scattered leaves in the hope that all these good deeds would alleviate the misery weighing down my soul in this life and the next.

Day after day I went to work, then to the temple, and then home, until one day I dedicated myself to the nunnery and was given the title "*Huyn Phúc*" ("dark happiness"). Life didn't seem to change; the restlessness in me only kept growing. Why was I given that title? "Huyn" means "black" or "dark", and happiness ("Phúc") was nowhere to be found. Now I had been given that title, would it be my fate to never be able to get out of the darkness of this life?

The worries of this life were already such a misery to me, but the worries about the next life were like a nightmare that kept haunting me. In despair I thought to myself, "This life is so dreadful that death would be better." Many times I would sit in front of a bag of rat poison, thinking to myself, "Take courage! Death is good!" But I never had enough courage.

One sunny afternoon, I was cycling alone on the quiet Nguyen Du street. Above me was the vast sky, and before me was the dazzling road. I felt so small and alone in the middle of this expanse. I pedalled aimlessly, each turn of the wheel as sorrowful as the wheel of my life. Tears of self-pity started to fall. Under the blazing sun, I lifted my watery eyes up to the sky and pleaded earnestly, "O God of Heaven! If you are real, please save me! I'm so miserable." I cannot understand why I went to the temple every day but I called out to "God" in times of trouble and not to Buddha. I was in the pits of loneliness and hopelessness. When I cried out "O God!" something snapped in my soul.

My neighbour often shared stories and testimonies about God, but I would get annoyed. I thought to myself, "Doesn't she have anything else to talk about besides God?" My religious pride stopped me from wanting to listen to her and made me hate what she said. But after a lot of debating within my own mind, I decided to approach my neighbour whom I used to avoid. Trying to choke back my sobs, I said, "Thuy, I don't know why I'm so miserable. Can I go with you to church this Sunday?"

I could see the excitement in her eyes. Her boyfriend said, "Ms Phuoc, I can sense your restlessness. God said in the Bible, 'Come to me, all you who are weary and burdened, and I will give you rest'."

Amazed, I wondered silently, "Is that what it really says? Weary and burdened, that's exactly how I'm feeling."

That night I continued to ponder on Thuy's boyfriend's words. If you see someone suffering, you would usually just say "poor you". Who would ever want to carry another's burden! But the Bible said to bring our burdens to find rest. It was so strange. I was anticipating and looking forward to church on Sunday. Thank God that that Sunday was the day I truly laid my burdens down. Although it has been more than twenty years, I remember clearly my first impression of sitting in a pew at Tuy Ly Vuong Church. There were friendly faces, melodies from the piano, and a gentleness that was so different from the dark and smoky environment I was in every day. Behind the pulpit were words in huge print: "Who is Jesus?" I whispered those words to myself; they were voicing the very question in my heart.

It was a special day in my life — the day I learned about Jesus, the Son of God, who came to die for sinful persons, including me. No one could ever love me as much as He does. Like a flooded dam, I could not stop my tears from falling in amazement. My tears were previously on account of my soul's burdens; now my tears washed away all my sorrow.

Who can wipe away the dark clouds of my life besides God? The joy and peace that I had never experienced didn't just last for a day, a week, or a month. It has lasted for twenty years. God did not bring me out of my circumstances; everything around me is still the same. But He transformed my heart, from being sorrowful to joyful. I have finally found the purpose for my life, and God gives me great pleasure in sharing His Good News to others. In fact, one day, the director at my work place asked, "Are you here to work or to evangelise?"

I smiled and replied, "Both, sir!"

If I had not met Jesus, I would have died in misery in this life and the next. That is the reason I constantly want to tell others about Him. There is a fire burning inside me that I must share. It is He who gives me the privilege to learn His Word and serve Him. I can now count the great joy and many blessings He has given me.

For a long time, I lifted up to God a desire of my heart. I asked, "God, where is my other 'half'?" I kept waiting. Every time I received a wedding invitation, I would hold it in my hand and ask, "God, when will it be my turn to send others my wedding invitation?" Years went by. I grew older but my hope never grew dim. If anyone asked if I had a prayer request, I would share with no hesitation: "Please ask God to let me meet my other half." I was honest with God and my close friends about my wish. Even though there were times I felt discouraged, I continued to wait in confidence:

All kinds of animals have pairs,
but where is my pair?
Lord, I have been waiting for so long.
I'm worried that my hair will turn from black to grey,
But I'm thinking again, it's alright, Lord —
My gracious Father will fulfil my desire.

Fifteen years of waiting is truly a long time. I was inspired by the story of the wedding at Cana. I believed that the longer God let me wait, the more incredible His gift would be for me. It is true that no one who hopes in the Lord will ever be put to shame (Psalm 25:3). God is faithful, He loves me, saved me, and exceeds my deepest needs.

God chose for me an Australian Christian, who was so many miles away, to be my husband. At first, there seemed to be great difficulties. However, the barriers of language, height, and weight were no longer a problem, for God was the One who had brought us together. The deep love my husband has for me is a reason to thank God each day.

I cannot recount all the amazing things He has done through the marriage that He let me wait a long time for. I've learned a lot through that. God always has His perfect timing. There is nothing too difficult for Him and He knows what is best for my life. I am truly satisfied in His loving arms.

Today, I see my son
walking home with his
mattock, chatting happily
with the neighbours and
sharing how
God had healed
and saved him.

Out of Madness

Phuong Vi, based on the testimony of Ba Nho

I was born and grew up in Vinh Long. After getting married, I gave birth to two sons and four daughters. Unfortunately, my oldest son, Thanh Van Nguyen, had a mental illness when he was about eighteen years old. He had to quit school when he was in the sixth grade due to our family's finances. Up to the age of fifteen or sixteen, he lived a normal life as any other youth. But after he turned eighteen, he became very aggressive. He would wander around and sometimes beat up family members. Our family had to live with that for many years without any solution. Many times we requested that the police put him in jail, but they soon sent him home because they did not know what to do with him. We could not send him to Bien Hoa Mental Hospital because we did not even have enough money for rice. My husband was also sick and unable to work, while my other children were too young.

My son grew progressively crazier. He was quite a large-built person and he had such extraordinary strength. We had to run and hide every time he started beating people up. Nobody dared to stay in the house. Even my husband and I had to stay away. Many nights we slept in the bush or behind the banana trees in the garden. Frightened, the whole family decided to restrain and tie my son to a tree trunk. It was our only option. So one day we joined our efforts and used a rope to tie him to a four-season tree in the backyard.

He started to scream and yell violently when he realised that he was no longer free. Once, he managed to escape, and we had to chain him to the tree. He stayed there for months, through the hot and the cold weather. He ate and slept there, and it was also his restroom. When it rained heavily, he would curl up under the tree. My heart was broken but I could not do anything. I told myself, "He brought that upon himself; who can help him?"

After a while, my son refused any food or drink. We brought him three meals every day but he would kick the tray away and try to attack anyone within his reach. Nobody dared to go close to him. Everybody in the neighbourhood knew about my son's mental condition, and they asked us to approach different voodoo doctors, but no one was strong enough to restrain him and bring him anywhere. To be honest, deep down inside I hoped that he would die to escape from his suffering and be less of a burden for our family. The four-season tree died after four months, but he was still alive, so we had to move him over to the coconut tree.

❧

Besides farming, I also gathered shellfish and crabs to sell at the market for some side income.

One day, it was almost sunset but my basket was still full, so I asked the lady selling shrimp paste next to me, "Could you please buy this basket of crabs so I will have some money to buy rice for my kids? We haven't had any since morning."

She replied with compassion that although she doesn't eat crabs she will buy them to help me. She also asked where I live because she wanted to visit us. At first I said that I live very far away, because I did not want anyone to see our crumbling house that my son had destroyed. Besides, my crazy son was in the backyard — sometimes he would lie still under the tree, but most of the time he would be yelling and screaming horribly. But since she was so earnest, I had to tell her the truth.

Although my house was quite a distance away, the lady walked home with me.

She gladly entered our empty home with the broken roof. I could feel that she cared, so I took her out to the back and pointed to my son. Seeing my son's scrawny body and his wounded leg — which he had injured when he struggled to break free — she stepped forward. She did not show fear or run away like other people.

"How long has he been tied up like that?" she asked.

I sighed and replied, "About eight months."

"Only God can save your son, but first you need to accept Jesus because you are his mum."

She explained to me about God and encouraged me to trust Him. I agreed because I didn't have any other choice. She led me to pray to invite Jesus into my heart.

After that, she walked with me to where my son was tied up. I saw her whispering something as she approached my son, then she said to him with a loud voice, "Jesus loves you very much. Would you believe in Him, Thanh?"

He nodded.

"I'm going to untie you now and you have to behave, okay?" she asked.

My son nodded excitedly. It had been a long time since he could talk. He was only able to scream.

She turned to me and asked me to help her untie him so that she could bring him to her house and pray for him. She asked me for my permission to do so. I could not believe what my ears had just heard. I looked at her — she was a normal woman just like me, a village woman. How could she dare to do what neither the police nor a group of people would attempt.

I was stunned, but nodded and followed her lead.

The chains were rusty and the lock could not be opened. So she and I, two women in their late fifties, started to saw off the chain from the coconut tree. My whole family watched from afar; no one dared to come near. Eventually, the chains fell off.

The lady took my son to the nearby pond. His body was so emaciated that it looked like he was all bones covered with skin. She kept repeating, "In the Name of Jesus, please save him, God!"

She washed him from head to toe. To my amazement, my son listened obediently to her. Then she took him inside to give him a haircut and trimmed his fingernails and toenails. She told me to bring him a clean set of clothes and something to eat.

She asked if she could bring him home to live with her for a while until he fully recovered. I did not know how to reply. I wanted her to take him away for good, but I did not dare say anything because I was afraid she would know my true intentions.

So she took him home, with the chains still dangling around his leg. He actually let her hold his hand as they walked. I came out of my shock and ran after them to give her the medication that we used to give him every time he acted up. She refused, "No, you should just take that back, he doesn't need medication."

I looked at the woman who was wearing a palm-leaf hat. She had a basket of shrimp-paste on one side and my son on the other. Their shadows gradually disappeared into the distance.

I walked home speechless, both happy and scared at the same time. I could not believe what had just happened. I even ran to the back to look at the coconut tree to make sure it was real, that my son was no longer there. My husband and I could not sleep that night; we were preparing ourselves to be called by the police or scolded by people for letting our son loose. I honestly thought that he would beat up someone that night.

But then a day passed, and then two, three days, and I didn't hear any news about my son! The lady brought him back after two weeks. He was in good health and no longer aggressive. He could even recognise and greet us with "mum" and "dad". Everyone in the village came to see him. When they looked at the lady, they said to one another, "This lady is scary, she must have a very powerful amulet to be able to control that guy!"

My son did not want to return home, but asked to stay with her forever. She smiled and explained to me, "Our family would like to take him in, but our house is so small, and we also have a daughter. It's not convenient for him to live there. I'm sending him back to you, but I will visit regularly."

She taught me how to lay my hands on him and pray for him in Jesus' Name whenever he acted up, and God would help him become normal again.

She kept her promise, regularly visiting my son and teaching him God's Word. She was not welcomed readily by everyone in my family, though. There were many rumours and doubts about her motives. Some thought that my family had been tricked into this, and even I was swayed.

My husband's relatives were particularly opposed to her. They said, "Of course he would become normal after being crazy for a while. What kind of god would make him crazy to heal him? And why is it that other crazy people are not healed by this god? Besides, what are doctors and pharmacists for? We have spent so much money and medication on him, that's why he's fine now."

However, the lady still patiently came, and was kind even to those who harassed her verbally.

After some time, my family came to believe in God. There were nine of us: my husband and me, our children, and a few nephews and nieces. We started a Bible class at our home. After that, our neighbours accepted Christ, and a church was formed. Our house became a place for worship every Sunday.

God gradually brought our family out of extreme poverty. We were able to build a tile-roofed house, which is brighter and cleaner. The wet dirt floor has now been replaced with Chinese tiles.

I thank God that my son has been well for three years now. Only much later did I discover that she had brought my son to a prayer meeting in Tra On, which is eleven kilometres away from our home, that very night. The church was having a fast for three days. My son arrived on the second day. Because of his condition, they all decided to fast longer to pray for his healing before sending him to her home.

After I accepted God, I had the privilege of attending one of those monthly prayer meetings. The lady had told me that praying for my son was very important, and that I needed to learn how to pray for him.

Today, I see my son walking home with his mattock, chatting happily with the neighbours and sharing how God had healed and saved him. He is now thirty-three years old, making a good living as a hired hand in the field. Whenever someone asks if he wants to get married, he would reply, "Not yet, I need to save up money to help my mum first."

God had mercy on my son and on me. In those dark days, I callously wanted to kill my own son. But God had a plan for his life, so that my family could be witnesses and tell of His amazing power. I am truly grateful to Him.

The hospital became her home... She had to go to the hospital regularly to have her blood filtered. She could not be away from the city and medical support because it was a matter of life and death to her.

The Winter is Gone
Cloud

She was a tall and pretty girl, but there was an unmistakable sadness in those black eyes of hers.

When Quyen-Nga turned twenty-one, the hospital became her home. Nga's kidneys had failed and she was unable to urinate like normal people can. She had to go to the hospital regularly to have her blood filtered. She could not be away from the city and medical support because it was a matter of life and death for her.

Many a night she would sit in the dark, feverish and gasping for air, with no one to comfort her. At times, looking at her peers who were full of youthful vitality, she felt completely depleted. Life was so dark and devastating to Nga.

Her parents loved her very much and were also devastated by her health condition. They often brought her to the temple to pray for her. But everything seemed hopeless.

There were some afternoons when her eyes would be full of tears as she realised that all her deepest dreams and even little delights were quietly leaving her. The day she told her boyfriend about her condition was also the day she felt her relationship starting to go south. She could only cry silently.

She was constantly wrestling with the pain, and the suffering was so great that she even thought of suicide. "*Would that be an escape for me?*" she wondered. Tossing and turning at night, she would often dream of a tranquil and isolated place where nobody knew her. Sad and confused, she wanted to become a Buddhist nun so that she could find peace.

A year went by, and she got to know a friend over the Internet. He would talk to her about God. She learned that he, too, had had a life full of disappointment and discouragement. He used to be a drug addict but was now set free from his addiction. He confessed to her that God is the only hope and security he has.

Nga was chatting with him one afternoon when she was feeling distressed, and he asked her to look up a lady by the name of Thu, who was very dear to him.

Nga figured that she had nothing to lose and decided to contact Thu. Nga was greeted with a friendly and gentle voice. Thu told Nga about the One who truly loves her, and that if she decided to receive His love, she would experience real joy and peace that comes from Him. Her eyes wide with surprise, Nga wondered, "Can that really be true?"

There was a big change in Nga's life after that conversation. Thu was like a second mother who supported and guided her in her walk with God. Strangely, all her dark and negative thoughts had disappeared and she realised the amazing truth that God is the hope and purpose that she had been searching for.

Those black eyes are no longer sad but sparkling with joy. Instead of being bogged down by depression because of her sickness, she gladly goes out to share the Good News to others.

Looking at her, I can't help but say, "Nga, you look totally different from the first time I saw you."

She smiled, her long, smooth hair swept aside, "God did it!"

Jesus is so amazing. Even though Nga cannot cure her illness, her existence each day is a miracle. Simply by looking at her appearance, one can hardly tell that she is critically ill. She has a ruddy complexion and is happy, while others with the same illness look pale and tired. Many of them have passed on, too.

But more than anything, Nga has experienced God. Her heart has been changed. He has turned her restlessness into peace and her grief into joy.

On 21 March 2010, Quyen-Nga experienced another blessing from God. It was the day she married Tuan. It was a happy day not only for the young couple, but also for the many people who love, care, and pray for her.

Many had thought of Nga's getting married as something "unimaginable" because of her illness. But with God's providence, the young couple has been married for almost two years now. They are full of happiness, serving God wholeheartedly even with all the ups-and-downs in life. More than anyone else, Nga understands that life is short, and it is her hope, together with her husband, to make the best of every opportunity to bless the lives around them.

When I asked Tuan about his marriage, he only smiled and said, "The more I get to know Nga, the more I admire her. She has such amazing vigour."

That "amazing vigour" can only come from a heart that fully relies on God. A normal, healthy person who lives without His strength would still be weak.

May Nga be healed by His wounds (Isaiah 53:5) so that she will continue to be an amazing and wonderful testimony of God's love.

> "… but those who hope in the LORD will renew their strength.
> They will soar on wings like eagles;
> they will run and not grow weary,
> they will walk and not be faint."
> (Isaiah 40:31)

I went to church feeling uneasy because of the thought that I might have been tricked into this. But strangely, the lyrics described exactly how I felt, so I opened my mouth and joined the singing.

Thanksgiving

Hieu Thi Le

I was awoken by the babbling sound of Thien An in her sleep. She smiled, hugged me, and fell right back into her peaceful sleep. Perhaps she was having a pleasant dream. I whispered into her ear, "Continue your sweet dream, okay, baby? We have a heavenly Father watching over us; He will fulfil your dream just as he has in my life."

Indeed, the life that my daughter and I have today is a dream come true. It's something that we can never explain, for by faith and prayer, God saved me from gripping fear.

I do not know the source of my unfathomable shame. Perhaps it was from those times that I blindly engaged in spirit play and worship, or the thing called "meeting people from the underworld". Every night, a dark spirit overtook me and was intimate with me. During those long years, I was fearful and tired, my body was exhausted and without life. I wanted to be set free but I could not do anything. Each day went by, and I felt both disgust and pity towards myself. I had seen many fortune tellers and voodoo doctors to make offerings, atonements, and prayers in the hope of being delivered from the bondage I was in.

I was a Catholic, and went to church every Sunday for confession, asking Mary to save me. But not only did things remain unchanged, the problem became more and more serious.

As fate ordained it, I got married to Sam Dinh Do in 1997. I was happy, but only for a short while.

When I became pregnant with my first child, the ghost appeared to me every night. It threatened to choke the foetus to death. In my sleep I often saw monstrous dark shadows coming to terrify me and take away my baby. I had a miscarriage soon after that. I felt torn between the real world and the demonic one. I was groping in a spiritual darkness that was like a prison, confining my life.

After a while, I became pregnant again, and gave birth to my second child. Life was still a horrifying battle. Our family's finances grew tighter. I had to take up many different jobs for money to raise our children. No matter how hard I tried, I could never lessen the burden and distress.

Our family decided to go back to An Khe, my husband's hometown. Because life was rough, my husband fell into drinking, and I was the one bearing the effects of his drunkenness. He would rain down beatings unreasonably on my children and me. Three to four times a month, the police would have to take him to their station, and he would promise to stop the violence. But soon enough, everything would go back to normal.

Unable to bear such a life, I thought of killing my husband, who constantly harassed me, and then ending my own life to stop the terror.

Being financially crippled, spiritually defeated, and mentally depleted made me ill. My head would throb with pain whenever I was exposed to light, and all strength would leave my body. I attempted suicide many times, but was unsuccessful.

One day, my neighbour and friend Diep came to visit me. After hearing my story, she said, "Hieu, you should come to Christ. Only He can save you."

I refused. I said, "I used to ask God many times, but nothing happened."

Diep then invited a lady to visit me. She patiently told me about the power and love of God, and invited me to church. I went to church feeling uneasy because of the thought that I might have been tricked into this. But strangely, the lyrics described exactly how I felt, so I opened my mouth and joined the singing. Peace began to take over my overwhelming fear. I accepted God that very Sunday.

The first rain of the season brought along a raging storm. The road to my home was filled with mud and water. But the lady showed up every night to teach me from the Bible about God, and His love and salvation for me.

The dark spirit, however, would angrily appear to me, "You have to kick that woman out of this house or I will kick you out!"

Once while I was lying on the hammock, it somehow flipped me out and sent me rolling out of the door.

I was so afraid that I did not dare to continue learning God's Word, but the lady told me, "This is a battle. If you want to live peacefully with God, you need to have His Word and study it."

I decided to risk it! The more I studied God's Word, the more my mind was renewed. The dark spirit was gone and I did not even notice its absence. My sickness was also gone. My health and countenance improved each day.

Initially, my husband strongly opposed my decision to believe in God and go to church to worship Him. But after seeing the changes in me, he also decided to come to Christ.

For two years, our family has lived in the love of God and of the church. God brought me spiritual mentors, mothers, and loving friends who guided me in applying His Word in my daily life. I saw some changes in my husband, as he became more responsible towards the family. We decided to have another child. Those were the good years of our marriage.

In preparing for our newborn, my husband went to Binh Thuan to look for work that paid better. Being far away from church, not studying God's Word, and living among a faithless community slowly distanced him from the Christian faith. Temptations swept him back to his old ways. As a result, he not only came home without a dime in his pocket, but he was also in a worse condition than before. It was painful for me to find out that he was in a relationship with another woman, a fact that he didn't even try to hide from me.

He was not the one who brought me to the hospital to deliver my baby. Instead, it was Diep and the lady. The one who provided for us was not my husband, but Jesus. He was also the One who comforted and lifted me up. During that storm of life, the lady named my baby girl "Thien An" or "grace". No matter how bad my situation was, I always believed that His grace was in my life.

Come Easter 2006, my heart was heavy. I began to fast and pray for my husband. He raged at me when he found out that I was fasting for him. He cursed me and blasphemed against God. He became the old person that he used to be, abusing me physically, and kicking me out of the house.

I quickly grabbed a few sets of clothes and left with my two children. Only much later did I realise that that was the moment God had liberated my life, just as He brought the Israelites out of slavery.

Through the many years of ups and downs, trying to raise two children on my own, He always reached out His hand to help and guide me. He led me step by step as I moved to Binh Duong to take a job as a security guard for Sao Viet Shoe Manufacturer. I truly experienced His promise in Psalm 23:2, "He makes me lie down in green pastures, he leads me beside quiet waters".

I rented a small room, which became a shelter for the three of us. There was no more fear of abuse. God provided me with a scooter to go to church and send my kids to school and back. I am very satisfied with our current condition. I draw a small salary but it is enough to feed, clothe, and school my children. I love my church and we go there every Sunday, even though the journey is long and sometimes inconvenient. My children are thriving in the love and care of the church.

My daughter Thien An is now four years old and my older son, thirteen. God healed Thien An from a serious asthma condition that I thought would only lead to death. He has answered so many of my earnest pleas. How can I not give Him thanks? Every night I talk to Him and sing this hymn:

> "Amazing grace
> How sweet the sound
> That saved a wretch like me
> I once was lost, but now I'm found
> Was blind, but now I see."
> (John Newton)

Thank God that He
rose again so that my
dead marriage could
come alive in Him.

Speaking Words of Forgiveness

Binh Thi Trinh

For twenty-five years our family life was hell on earth. My husband was drunk almost every day, and the first person he would brutally beat up after coming home was his wife. I was the one who had to bear his remorseless beatings. Even when I was pregnant with my first child, he would whip me with an electric wire every time we disagreed. I was terrified, and had to beg him for forgiveness because I was afraid that he might hit the baby inside me. He would laugh it off and make me crawl around the house without spilling a cold bucket of water on my back. He seemed to enjoy this new game of his. Holding a whip on one hand he would say, "I will beat you up if you spill the water!"

At times I was hung in the middle of my lawn to be beaten up for everyone to see. In those lonely days I had no one to defend or protect me. Although my neighbours saw what my husband did to me, nobody dared to say anything. He continued to come up with all sort of cruel things to satisfy the animal in him.

I was hoping that one day my husband would change, or perhaps when my kids grew up they would be able to defend me. But it turned out that my husband would beat up both me and my children. Some days, after beating us up, he would block the doors with barbed wire that was plugged into an electric outlet so that no one could come in or go out. That was our life — we never had a day of peace and never received anything good from my husband. Whether sober or drunk, he was always violent and cruel. We had four children and our lives were filled with agony. My children even plotted to murder their father so that they would not have to live with him. But they failed, and life went on.

My only job is selling things at the market. A friend who saw my miserable situation shared with me about God. I was already at the end of the road, so one day I went with her to a church nearby, and I prayed to accept Him. The church pastor said, "I am very sorry about your situation, but we really don't know what to do for you. Only God can help you."

My spirits were lifted every time I went to church. I had to sneak out every Sunday to go there, afraid that I might get killed if my husband found out. After testing the waters for a while and observing that my husband did not seem to oppose the idea, I summoned up the courage to ask the pastor to come and share about God to him.

Surprisingly, he accepted God at their first encounter. After believing in God, he continued to get drunk but grew less violent, and gradually he changed. Our neighbours were very curious because they did not hear him yelling and cursing. Even a police officer, who was once thrown into the river by him, was very impressed and asked, "Oh, is that you Mr Thom? You seem different lately!"

Since then, many good things started to happen in our family, but our marriage was still broken, even though my husband became aware of his wrongdoings after believing in God. He would sometimes hug me and call me "dear" instead of using the usual curse words. At other times he would hold my hands tight, as if he was about to say something sweet, but I was turned off and disgusted. I could not and would never forgive him because he had been so cruel to us. I thought that I had the right to not forgive him.

However, as I continued to walk with God and listen to His Word at every church service, I realised that my marriage could not continue in hatred.

One day, we decided to go for a marriage seminar. There were about thirty-four other couples attending the seminar. During one of the workshops, the instructors encouraged us to sit next to each other, hold hands, apologise to, and pray for one another. It was impossible for me to hold his hand! I turned away to avoid looking at him and the other couples who were more fortunate. I believed that I could not forgive this person. Wasn't it enough that I now knew God and was moving on with life, without divorce or abuse?

On the second day, we learned about intimacy in marriage. The men and the women went to different rooms. Many women shared about their lives, and I started to sob. I shared with the others about the deepest hurt in my life. I cried and asked them to pray for me because I was not able to forgive my husband. Many wept with me, and the class was quiet for a long time.

Then the instructor said gently, "It upsets me to hear your story. Is it true that you cannot forgive him for all the cruelty? But Binh, my dear sister, we don't have the right to choose. The Word of God in Luke 6:27 tells us, 'Love your enemies, do good to those who hate you'. You do not just need to forgive him but also love him. But thank God that we can do what He asks of us by His strength and not by our own. Now we will all pray for you and ask God for that kind of strength."

Another sister piped up, "Sister Binh, your husband's actions before he came to Christ were controlled by the devil. But he now belongs to God. He is a new creation; you should forget about the old Mr Thom. Now he is the new Mr Thom — you even admitted that he has changed, right?"

I sat down in the middle of the room, and all the women immediately gathered around me, laid their hands on me, and in tears, cried out to God on my behalf. I had never met most of them before, but they still prayed for me with all their hearts, crying, and hugging me. There is truly nothing more precious than the sisterhood we have in Christ.

While they were praying, I felt something strange happening within me. It was something that I had never experienced before. It was the love of the Father, the love of God which filled me in such a powerful way.

After dinner that same evening, my husband and I took a walk under the moonlight at the suggestion of the instructors. We walked to a quiet place where we were alone, and I held his hand and told him the decision of my heart and mind, "I love you and I forgive you. We are now one in Christ."

My husband could not say a word but was holding my hand ever so tightly. Under the moonlight I could see tears running down his cheeks. After we said a prayer together, he called home to tell our children that I had forgiven him.

Today, we live together bound by a love that I never thought we would have. God changed my husband, and he became a servant of God. Because of the changes in my family, many people from my neighbourhood have come to believe in God. Just as the Word of God says, "By this everyone will know that you are my disciples, if you love one another" (John 13:35). Thank God that He rose again so that my dead marriage could come alive in Him.

It's truly amazing to experience God and have His love overflow in my heart. I would like to quote Paul the apostle to describe my gratitude to Him: "Thanks be to God for his indescribable gift!"

Giving Praise to God

Thu-Huyen, Nguyen

"I envy brother Quang and sister Huyen. Just look at how happy they are together!"

That's a compliment we often get. At times like this we would turn and look at each other. We did not have an easy time getting to where we are today.

Eight years ago, I was a young and spirited girl. I had recently broken up with my previous boyfriend and was tired of the lack of freedom in my family, so I agreed to marry Quang although we had only known each other for less than two months. My decision for a lifetime commitment was made so carelessly. I felt indifferent on my wedding day, as if it were somebody else's.

Conflict was unavoidable in our marriage. The frequency of our arguments and quarrels escalated after I gave birth to my firstborn. There was no love, and life was nowhere near how I dreamt it to be. I was utterly discontented with everything and started to question the reason I married Quang.

During that time, my mum came to know God and accepted Christ. Since my husband and I lived at my parents' place, we decided to do the same. This one event brought many changes to my mum's life. Rejoicing and trusting in God, she dedicated herself to prayer, and decided to get rid of the ancestral altar in the house. I did not argue and simply regarded it as something that had to be done.

Four months later, my dad passed away due to an illness, and there were rumours that my mum was being punished for abandoning the altar. Influenced by my in-laws, I began to treat her harshly. We argued so much that we did not want to see each other anymore. I cast my Bible aside and cut off all contact with my friends at church. My mum and I grew distant, as if we were thousands of miles apart, whereas in actual fact we lived very near each other. Deep down in my heart, I held hatred towards my mum as well as those who were involved in her decision to destroy our ancestral altar.

I was very discontented with my marriage and all my relationships. Although my family was well-off and we led a comfortable life, I never felt peace and contentment in my heart. I was disoriented, losing faith in myself, and not knowing what to hope for in life. I even left home to live by myself. I wanted space for my husband and me to think about whether we should continue or end our lifeless marriage.

After living like that for a while, I returned home only to discover that the tension between us had worsened. Each day was filled with arguments and quarrels. Even though at first he attempted to love me wholeheartedly, he became disappointed when he realised he would never have a place in my heart, no matter how much he tried. He turned to gambling to fill the emptiness and to feed the false hope that the money he won would eventually bring happiness to our lives. But our home and marriage was really broken. I no longer wanted to have a life like that, and I thought of divorce many times.

Some days, I would bump into my mum on the streets, but we acted no differently from two strangers. I looked at her with eyes full of hatred and I did not want to talk to her. What I didn't know was that during that one year of conflict, my mum had been changed dramatically by God. She spent hours praying for my family each day. God eventually answered my mum's consistent prayers, and I am still amazed at what He did.

One afternoon, a Christian friend of mine stopped by my sugarcane juice stall to return me my Bible, which she had found in her closet. I had to accept it because it belonged to me. I left it in the drawer at the stall because I did not know where else to put it. Once in a while, when business was slow, I would take it out to read.

After almost a year and a half of bitterness and harshness towards my mum, I had an urge to reconcile with her. It was the full-moon festival then, so I bought a box of moon cakes and had my sister-in-law accompany my daughter to bring it to her grandma.

My daughter started visiting my mum more often. Every time she came back from her grandma's, my daughter would tell me non-stop, "Mummy, you've got to thank God!" At first I pretended that I didn't hear her, but my four-year-old was persistent. All day long she tried to come up with all kinds of things to make me thank God for. Many times when I was busy preparing sugarcane juice for customers, she would come next to me, saying, "Mummy, you've got to thank God; you have to!" Because I didn't want to be bothered and wanted to keep her hands away from the grinder, I would give in, "Yes, thank God! I thank You, God!"

Although I said those words casually, it seemed that God used them to chip off my stubbornness bit by bit. Through my little girl, my husband and I eventually reconciled with my mum. We then started to attend church regularly again.

God changed my husband and me through the Bible studies. We realised our sinful condition by the truth of His Word. I was surprised to find out that I so often went against what was taught in the Bible, and that was the source of the problems in my life. Thank God that after we learned about

His truth we — as a married couple — were able to turn around from our wrongdoings. And like His mercies that are "new every morning", I began to realise that my love for my husband was growing each day. It was a miracle.

I cannot finish telling about all the blessings of walking with Jesus. He not only changed our hearts but also our lives. What He has given and provided for my family exceeds what I have asked and wished for. From big things such as having a home to live in to small things such as choosing a good school for my daughter, we always see His loving hand working in our lives. He recently blessed us with another precious gift, our second child.

I used to be very discontented with all my relationships, but now I can thank Him for them. I fell in love with the same person I wanted to divorce and God healed the broken relationship with my mum. He also improved my relationship with my mother-in-law, and she eventually accepted Christ. Although she is a new believer, she has already started witnessing to her neighbour. It is truly amazing to experience God and have His love overflow in my heart. I would like to quote Paul the apostle in describing my gratitude to Him: "Thanks be to God for his indescribable gift!" (2 Corinthians 9:15).

Some people might like Fall, and others the seasons of Summer or Spring, but for me, I want to forever live in the Season of Praise.

He changed this evil heart and made it new". Truly, God changed the evil desire in me to kill my husband in revenge.

From War to Peace

Loan Thi-Kim Phan

I am the oldest child in a family that has been following Caodaiism for many years. My parents worked and settled in Trang Bang, Tay Ninh, where they donated land to build a Cao Dai temple. They kept a vegetarian diet all year round, but I was only vegetarian for the minimum ten days each month.

After the Vietnam War, my sister was sponsored to go to Canada to seek medical treatment for injuries she had sustained during the war. She remained there for college. Upon graduation, she worked in Cuba and married a Vietnamese there. I was occupied with making a living for myself and my family, and did not pay much attention to what was going on in her life. I received news about her mostly through the media, because she became an ambassador of UNESCO and travelled to many places around the world.

One day in 2004, my sister suddenly called me from Canada to tell me about Jesus and His salvation. We talked for a very long time. I listened for the sake of listening but did not understand anything at all. She suggested that I look for a church close by to find out more.

Our family was living in Cu Chi then, and I used to buy lemons and sell them at the market. God led me to Mr and Mrs Loan La from Hue. Mr Loan was my lemon supplier. Their home was also a gathering place for worship. With their help, I came to God and accepted Him as my Lord and

Saviour. I asked them for a Bible to read at home. Initially, the Bible was very difficult for me to understand, but with Mr Loan's instruction and my prayers for wisdom, God began to open my mind to understand what I read. I also enjoyed the fellowship with other believers in Cu Chi.

During that period, my family was in a lot of turmoil. I had recently undergone a gynaecological operation, and, as a result, my husband had an affair and neglected me. He was a communist officer, and after hearing that I was following God, he filed for divorce. The officers at the registry of marriage defended me because they knew that Christians are good people. However, my husband persisted in divorcing me. In confusion, I went to Mr Loan for advice. He told me not to divorce my husband because the Bible was against divorce.

I listened to Mr Loan, but at the same time there was a struggle inside me. I had bought ten litres of gasoline and planned to burn down the house of my "adversary", along with my husband. I did not care about the consequences. In fact, I considered twenty-five years of jail to be as bad as it could get.

But before I could carry out my plan, one day at twilight someone came to drop off my husband in front of our door and then ran away. My husband lay there like a dead person. It was only then that I found out that he had brain damage and needed dialysis. His mistress had abandoned him. My daughter and I brought him into the house and took care of him as if he had never forsaken us all these years. I read God's Word in Romans 12:17–21 and my heart was stirred by these verses: "Do not repay any evil for evil...Do not be overcome by evil, but overcome evil with good." I love the lyrics of Hymn 81 that says, "He changed this evil heart and made it new." Truly, God changed the evil desire in me to kill my husband in revenge.

Instead, I told him about God as I took care of him. But his heart was hardened and he did not want to believe. He passed away after fourteen months.

Nevertheless, I write these words today with praise that God has saved my life and my family's — including my parents and all my siblings. My eighth brother is currently serving at a church in Tan Chau (Tay Ninh). Thanks be to God that He could turn around the horrible Vietnam War and my sister's painful injuries, that she could come to know Him. And now my whole family is saved and at peace with God.

Thank you, Kim-Phuc, my sister. It was because of your phone call that I now know Jesus. I also believe that God worked out His plan of salvation for our family through you. May He continue to use you to bring many back to Him. Amen.

Acknowledgements

What you see recorded in this book is only a very small part of what God has done in our country, and we are very grateful to Him. He has given us the opportunity to work with the individuals in each story in this book. And because of their testimony our faith has been strengthened and we've gained great confidence in the power of God, who has never forsaken those who seek Him (Psalm 9:10). I hope you will also experience this loving and powerful God in each page of *Out of the Dark Night*.

The *Hat Muoi* editorial team would like to convey their warmest appreciation to John Maust and the Graceworks team. We are really grateful for all your help and encouragement to make the publication of this book a reality in order for it to bring blessings to many readers.

Dinh Thi Thanh Tin
On behalf of the *Hat Muoi* editorial team